Overlook School Library
Poughkeepsie, New York

DISCARDED

ABOUT THE BOOK

By using this book children can find out about different aspects of hot and cold. The author poses such questions as: On a hot sunny day, where is it best to sit—on a metal or wooden chair? What clothes are warmest? Which color clothing makes us feel cooler in the summer? Why do we rub our hands together to make them warm?

HOT & COLD presents many very simple experiments and projects for children. For instance, those concerned with the way water freezes and ice melts, the way heat travels from one thing to another, the way hot air rises, the way thermometers change as the temperature changes. As children do these projects and have the opportunity to make discoveries for themselves, they will know more about the world around them and have fun doing it. At the same time they will learn basic, new science concepts.

Lively, large, enjoyable illustrations accompany the text. They will also help the reader visualize the projects so that they may carry them out with greater success.

Also By Seymour Simon:

LET'S TRY IT OUT...WET & DRY
LET'S TRY IT OUT...LIGHT & DARK
LET'S TRY IT OUT...FINDING OUT WITH YOUR SENSES
DISCOVERING WHAT EARTHWORMS DO
DISCOVERING WHAT FROGS DO
DISCOVERING WHAT GOLDFISH DO
DISCOVERING WHAT GERBILS DO

And For Older Readers:

ANIMALS IN FIELD AND LABORATORY

LET'S-TRY-IT-OUT...
HOT & COLD
BY SEYMOUR SIMON

ILLUSTRATED BY JOEL SNYDER

McGRAW-HILL BOOK COMPANY

New York • St. Louis • San Francisco • Düsseldorf • Johannesburg
Kuala Lumpur • London • Mexico • Montreal • New Delhi • Panama
Rio de Janeiro • Singapore • Sydney • Toronto

For three Grandmothers: Rebecca, Clara, and Sadie

LET'S TRY IT OUT... HOT AND COLD
Copyright © 1972 by Seymour Simon and Joel Snyder. All Rights Reserved. Printed in the United States of America. No part of this publication may be reproduced, stored in a retrieval system, or transmitted, in any form or by any means, electronic, mechanical, photocopying, recording, or otherwise, without the prior written permission of the publisher

Library of Congress Catalog Number: 70-172033

The sun comes up early on the hottest day of the year.
The air is still.
A warm breeze blows through
the open windows of your room.

The morning delivery men call out to each other.
"Hot enough for you?"
"It's going to be a scorcher today."
"The temperature is already up to 80 degrees."

It's too hot for you to sleep any longer.
You get out of bed and dress.
Shorts, a light cotton shirt, socks, sneakers—
you don't need a jacket today!

After breakfast, you go outside to play.
The sun is higher in the sky than in the early morning.
The air is even hotter than when you awoke.
You bounce a ball and run a bit,
greet a friend and decide to sit down someplace.

You choose a place to rest:
in the sunlight or in the shade.
Which do you think is cooler?
Feel the ground where it is sunny.
Feel the ground where it is shady.
Which feels warmer to your skin?
Where will you feel cooler?

The sun is very hot.
Its rays warm the ground.
Touch some things in the sunlight:
the top of a car, the wall of a building,
a leaf, a rock, a lamppost, the hair on your friend's head.
How do they feel?

Place a baseball bat and a pair of roller skates
in a sunny spot.
Let them stay for a while, then feel them.
Which feels warmer?
Some things feel warmer than others
when the sun shines on them.
On a hot sunny day, which would you rather sit in:
a metal chair or a wooden one?

The sun climbs still higher in the sky.
It seems to hang almost overhead.
There's not much shade now.
The long shadows of early morning
are shorter in the noonday sun.

A friend's puppy sits with its tongue hanging out.
You call the pup to come and play.
"It's just too hot," its look seems to say.
Your friend looks at his puppy and laughs.
"It sure is hot today. The temperature must be
over 100 degrees."
It feels very hot on a summer day like this,
but how do you know what the temperature is?

Maybe you or your friend have a thermometer at home.
Some people place one just outside their window
so that they can read it from inside.

How hot or cold something is, we call its temperature.
A thermometer measures temperature
in numbers called degrees.
A thermometer usually has a colored liquid inside it.
When the air is warm, the colored liquid rises upward
in the tube of the thermometer.
When the air is cooler, the colored liquid moves downward
in the tube of the thermometer.

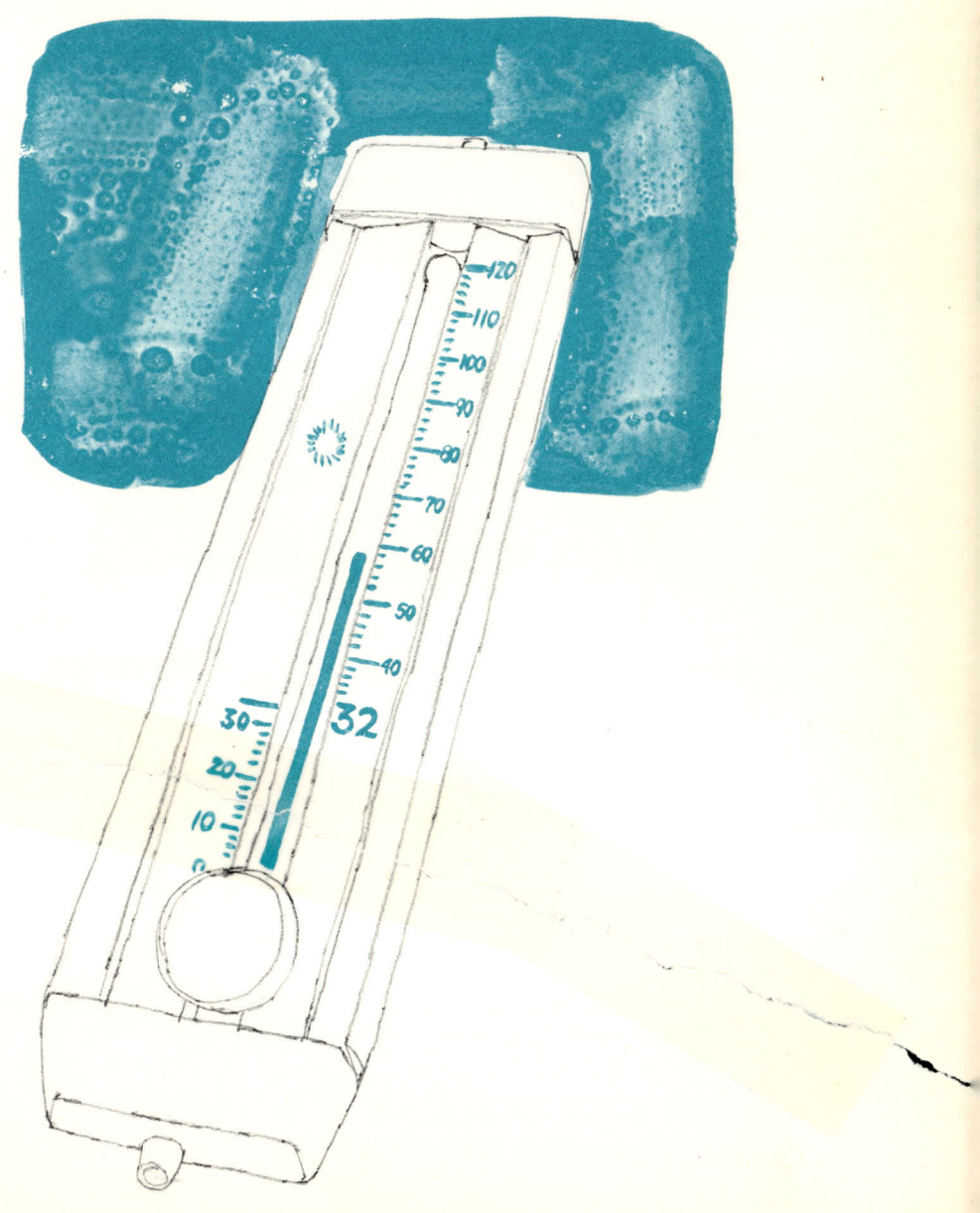

Try it out.
Place a thermometer in your refrigerator.
After a few minutes, take it out and mark the top of the liquid in the tube with a rubber band or a piece of tape.
Leave the thermometer out of the refrigerator for a few minutes.
Mark the top of the liquid in the tube now.
In which place was the liquid in the thermometer higher?

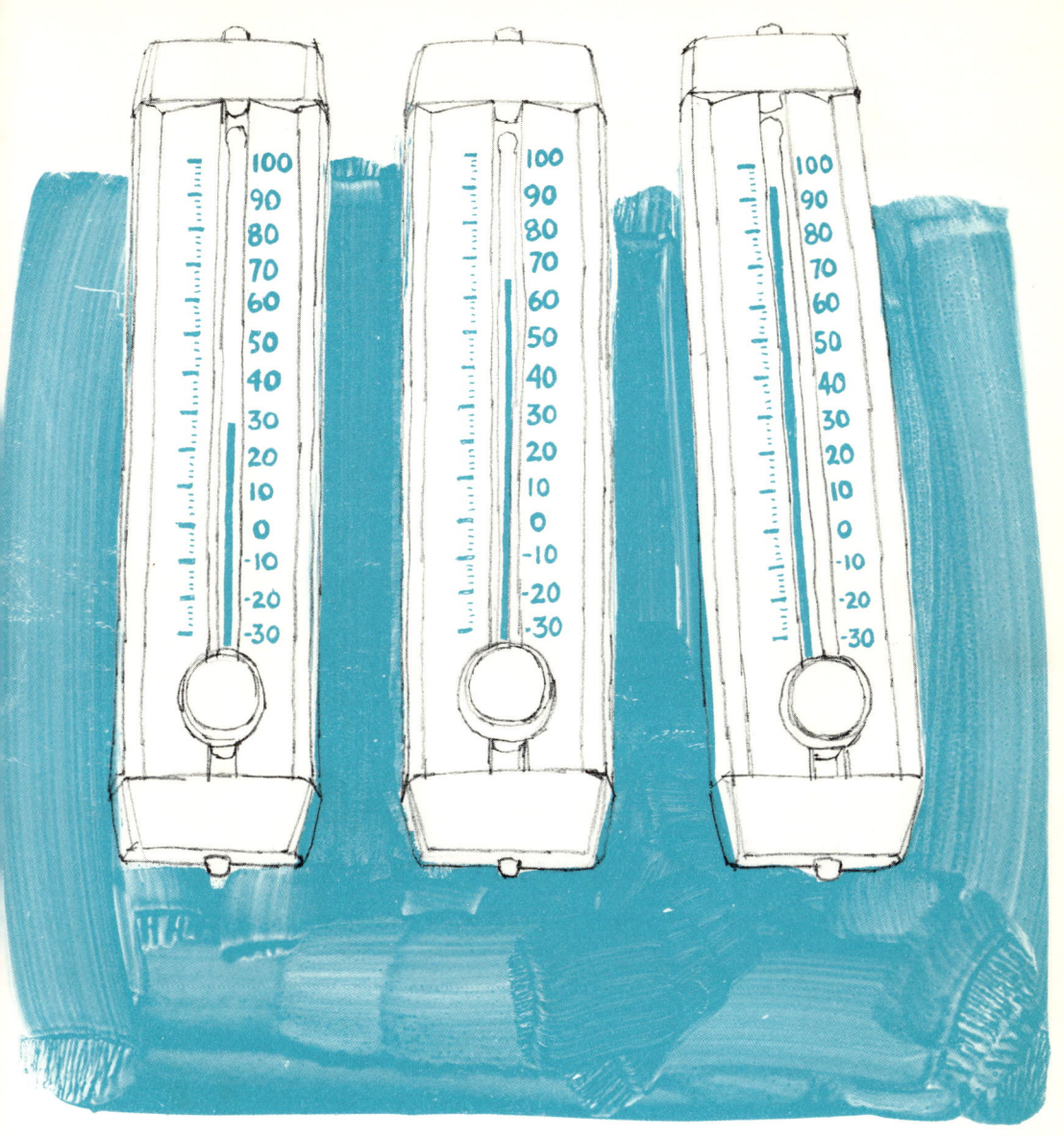

Thermometers help to tell us what kind of a day it is.
Look at these three thermometers.
Each shows air temperature on a different day during the year.
Which one shows a day when you might want to use your sled?
Which one shows a day when you might want to go swimming?
What would happen to the thermometer in the middle
if you put it into a glass of ice water?
What would happen if you put it into a glass of warm water?

A cold drink feels good on a hot summer day.
Would you like to make one for your friend?

Place a handful of ice cubes into a glass.
Fill it almost to the brim with water.
Stir the ice cubes around and around with a spoon.
What happens to the ice cubes as you stir them?

You can see hard wax soften
and melt too.
When a wax candle becomes warm enough,
it melts and turns to a liquid wax.
But wax must become much warmer than ice
for it to melt.

Even metals such as iron and steel melt
when they become very hot.
This happens in a blast furnace in a factory,
or with a welder's torch.

In the winter of the year,
you forget the summer's heat.
The crisp air makes your ears and nose tingle.
Frost forms on the window pane of your room,
and icicles hang from the branches of trees.
In the park, bundled-up boys and girls
skate on the frozen waters of the pond.

You pack a snowball and throw it as far as you can.
Even with gloves, your fingers are stiff and cold.
Can you think of how to make them warm?
Try this.
Take off your gloves and
rub your hands together.
How do they feel?
Press your hands together tightly and rub them faster.
How do they feel now?
Whenever one thing rubs against another,
it causes *friction*.

Friction can make things warm.
Rub two pieces of wood together.
How do they feel?
Scouts learn how to rub two pieces of wood together
so rapidly that they start a fire.
Friction also helps you to light a match.
Do you know how?

We make things warm in other ways too.
A gas flame on a stove warms up food.
An electric heater warms up the air in a room.
A roaring fire in a fireplace warms up
frozen fingers and toes on a cold winter day.
A hot cup of cocoa helps you warm up too.
Can you think of other things that are used
to give off heat?

Place some warm water in a pan.
Place the pan on a cool counter top in the kitchen.
Wait ten or fifteen minutes.
Feel the water.
How warm is it now?
Where did the heat in the water go?

Lift the pan and feel the counter top beneath.
The counter top feels warm.
Some of the heat went from the warm water
to the cool counter top.
Some of the heat went from the warm water
to the cooler air around it.
Heat always goes from hot things to cooler things.

Place the edge of a quarter or a half-dollar coin
into a cupful of very warm water.
What do you feel after a few seconds?
Heat travels easily through the metal coin
from the water to your fingers.
Place the edge of the coin against an ice cube.
Now what do you feel after a few seconds?
This time heat traveled through the metal coin
from your fingers to the ice cube.

Place the tip of a pencil into a cupful of very warm water.
Do you feel any heat coming through the wood?
Try placing the tip of the pencil against an ice cube.
Do your fingers feel cold?
Heat travels through some materials more easily than through others.
Heat travels easily through metal pots and pans to cook the food inside.
Heat doesn't travel easily through the wooden handle of a cooking spoon that you use to stir hot foods.

Heat also doesn't travel easily through wools and furs. Clothing made of wool and furs keeps your body heat from escaping on a cold winter day.

Drop a few small pieces of tissue paper
over a hot radiator.
Which way do they move?
The radiator heats the air near it.
The heated air moves upward.

Sometimes, outdoor fairs and circuses have a big,
brightly colored balloon.
The big balloon is filled with hot air.
What happens when they let it go?
When do you think it comes down?
Cool air is heavier than warm air.
The heavier cool air pushes up the lighter warm air.
In this way, heat travels
by putting the air in motion.

Hold your hand a few inches from the side
of an electric-light bulb.
Heat travels to your hand from the bulb
across the few inches of space.
In much the same way the rays of sunlight that warm the earth
travel across many miles of space.

During cold weather, you want the sun to warm you.
During hot weather, you want to stay cool.
What kind of clothing would you wear in the summer?
Does the material of the clothes you wear make a difference?
Let's try it out.
You will need two jars with tops, a wool sock and a cotton sock, and some warm water.
Pour warm water into each of the jars and close them tightly.

Pull the wool sock down around one of the jars.
Pull the cotton sock down around the other jar.
Wait ten minutes.

Feel the water in each of the jars.
Which sock helped keep the water warmer?
Which kind of sock would you wear when you go sleigh riding?
Which would you wear on the hottest day of the year?

What other materials are used in making your clothing?
Look at the labels inside.
If you can do the same experiments
with cloths of different materials,
use a rubber band to wrap the cloths
around the glass jars.

Does the color of your clothing make a difference?
Take a piece of black cloth and a piece of white cloth.
Both pieces should be made of the same kind of material.
Get two ice cubes from the refrigerator.
Place the ice cubes in a sunny spot.
Cover one with the white cloth and the other with the black cloth.
Which ice cube melts first?
Which color clothing would keep you cooler on a sunny day?

You like to be comfortable—
not too hot, not too cold.
Now you know how to warm up if you feel cold.
Now you know how to cool off if you feel warm.
Try it out.

ABOUT THE AUTHOR

SEYMOUR SIMON has been a science teacher for the last twelve years. He is a science book reviewer, has served as a science consultant, and has had over fifty articles published by Scholastic Publications. He has also written juvenile science books, including ANIMALS IN THE FIELD AND LABORATORY, DISCOVERING WHAT EARTHWORMS DO, DISCOVERING WHAT GOLDFISH DO, WET AND DRY, LIGHT AND DARK, and FINDING OUT WITH YOUR SENSES. A native New Yorker, he has done graduate work in psychology and biology. Mr. Simon lives in Great Neck, New York, with his wife and two boys.

ABOUT THE ARTIST

JOEL SNYDER, a native of Sunbury, Pennsylvania, has illustrated many children's books. He graduated from the Rhode Island School of Design. He now lives in Farmingdale, New York with his wife and two children.